Snap books

Friendship
Quizzes

Are You a Good Friend?

by Jen Jones

Consultant:
Stephanie Goerger Sandahl, MA, LPC
Clinical Specialist
Generations, Inc. Counseling Associates

CAPSTONE PRESS
a capstone imprint

Snap Books are published by Capstone Press,
151 Good Counsel Drive, P.O. Box 669, Mankato, Minnesota 56002.
www.capstonepub.com

 Books published by Capstone Press are manufactured with paper
containing at least 10 percent post-consumer waste.

Library of Congress Cataloging-in-Publication Data
Jones, Jen.
  Are you a good friend? / by Jen Jones.
    p. cm. — (Snap Books: Friendship quizzes)
  Summary: A quiz about loyalty.
  Includes bibliographical references and index.
  ISBN 978-1-4296-6541-4 (library binding)
  1. Friendship—Miscellanea—Juvenile literature. 2. Best
friends—Miscellanea—Juvenile literature. 3. Conduct of
life—Miscellanea—Juvenile literature. I. Title. II. Series.

BF575.F66J66 2012
177'.62—dc22   2010044634

Editor: Brenda Haugen
Designer: Veronica Correia
Media Researcher: Marcie Spence
Production Specialist: Laura Manthe

Photo Credits: Capstone Studio: Karon Dubke, cover, 1, 4 (bottom), 7, 9, 10, 11,
13, 14 (bottom), 15 (bottom), 22, 28; Shutterstock: Alexey Lysenko, 6 (bottom),
Alhovik, 15 (top), Alice (design element), Ayelet Keshet, (design element), azzzya,
(design element), BHodanbosi, 8 (right), blue67design (design element), Charla, 8
(left), Diamond_Images, cover (markers), Elise Gravel (design element), erwinova,
6 (top), gosn.Momcilo, 18, hans.slegers, 12, Jason Stitt, 27, Kateryna Larina, 15
(background), Maaike Boot, 17 (top), Maryloo, 14 (top), NemesisINC, 20,
Primusoid, 5, REDAV, 26, Tom&Kwikki, (design element), UltraViolet, 14
(background), Valua Vitaly, 24, zsooofija (design element),

Printed in the United States of America in Melrose Park, Illinois.
032011   006112LKF11

Table of Contents

Introduction

Do your friendships last through thick and thin? Or do you get going when the going gets tough? **Clichés** aside, the length and strength of your friendships speak volumes about your level of loyalty. Staying by a friend's side—through good times and bad—is what it's all about! Keeping your word is a big part of loyalty too. And the more loyal you are, the more **faith** your friends will have in you.

Want to discover whether you're a forever friend? This book is designed for you to do just that. Take this quiz to learn more about yourself and your relationships. From traitors to true-blue pals, you'll find all the answers about how loyal you really are. You'll also get ideas on how to be the greatest BFF you can be!

Even though this is nothing like taking a test at school (it's way cooler!), there are a few things you'll need before you get started. And don't worry—no #2 pencils required.

• Grab a sheet of notebook paper to write your answers down. You'll also need a pen or pencil. Number the sheet from 1 to 15, and you're ready to rock!

AND PLEASE, DO NOT WRITE IN THIS BOOK!!!

• Tell the truth. No one will see your answers but you.

OK ... ready, set, grow!

QUIZ

1- You win tickets to an awesome sold-out concert! The not-so-awesome part? It's on the same night as your BFF's b-day, and she wants to throw a beach bonfire. What do you do?

a) See if your friend wants to join you for the concert instead. After all, it would be a blast!

b) Sorry, but when the front row calls, you've got to answer! You'll make it up to her with a killer gift.

c) Give the tickets to your sibling and attend the party. Nothing comes between you and your BFF.

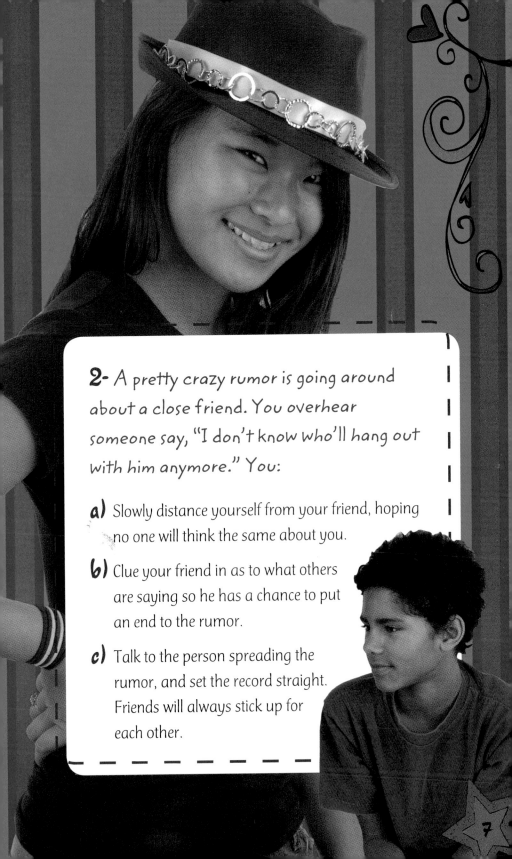

2- A pretty crazy rumor is going around about a close friend. You overhear someone say, "I don't know who'll hang out with him anymore." You:

a) Slowly distance yourself from your friend, hoping no one will think the same about you.

b) Clue your friend in as to what others are saying so he has a chance to put an end to the rumor.

c) Talk to the person spreading the rumor, and set the record straight. Friends will always stick up for each other.

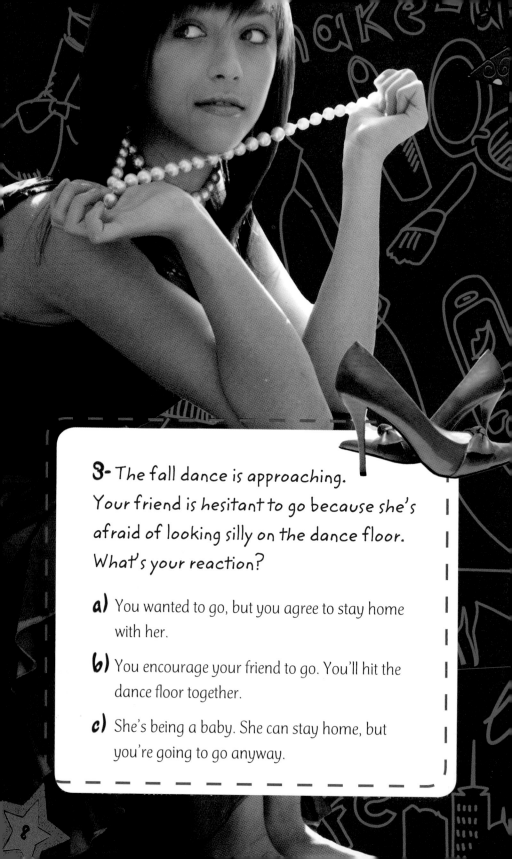

3- The fall dance is approaching. Your friend is hesitant to go because she's afraid of looking silly on the dance floor. What's your reaction?

a) You wanted to go, but you agree to stay home with her.

b) You encourage your friend to go. You'll hit the dance floor together.

c) She's being a baby. She can stay home, but you're going to go anyway.

4- Your friend wants to skip cheer practice and go shopping. She asks you to lie to the coach for her. What would you do?

a) Happen to "slip" and say where your friend is—in front of your coach. It's not fair that she gets to have all the fun!

b) Cover for her with the coach. After all, she'd do the same for you.

c) Say "no thanks." She'll have to talk to the coach on her own.

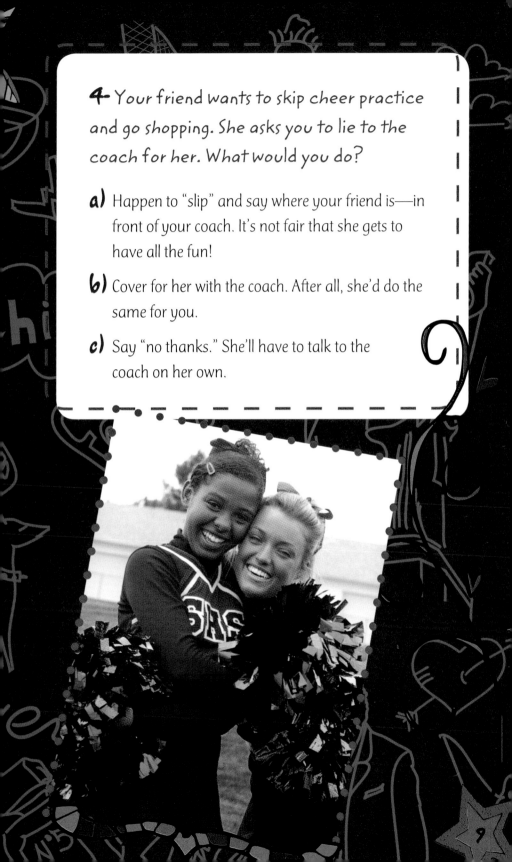

5- It's your turn to walk the dog after school. You promised your parents you'd do it. But you get invited to a popular girl's home after school. You've wanted an invite for ages and hate to turn it down. You:

a) Beg your brother to do doggie duty just this once.

b) Turn down the invite and walk your four-legged friend but pout the rest of the day.

c) Figure out a way to do both. You can't leave Fido hanging!

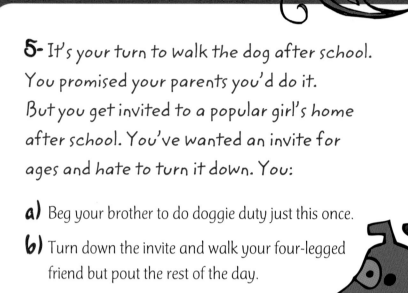

6- When you make a promise, it means:

a) You've got my word—unless my fingers are crossed!

b) I'll plan to do what I say, but if anything changes, I'll let you know.

c) The deal is sealed forever!

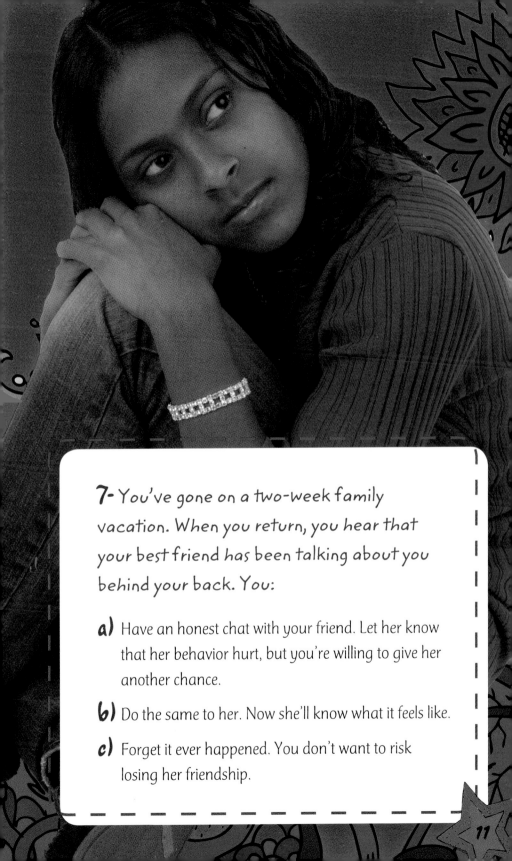

7- You've gone on a two-week family vacation. When you return, you hear that your best friend has been talking about you behind your back. You:

a) Have an honest chat with your friend. Let her know that her behavior hurt, but you're willing to give her another chance.

b) Do the same to her. Now she'll know what it feels like.

c) Forget it ever happened. You don't want to risk losing her friendship.

8- At a sleepover, the girls start pressuring you to spill another friend's secret. What do you do?

a) Stress out. You can't blab, but you don't want to disappoint your other friends either.

b) Tell them "no way!" A true friend never spills secrets.

c) Spill the beans, but make them swear it never leaves the room.

9- Your BFF from elementary school is moving back to town, but you now have a new best friend. You feel:

a) Annoyed. You hope she doesn't bring up little-kid stuff in front of your new BFF.

b) Excited. You can't wait to reconnect with your old friend.

c) Guilty. You hope she doesn't get upset with you for moving on.

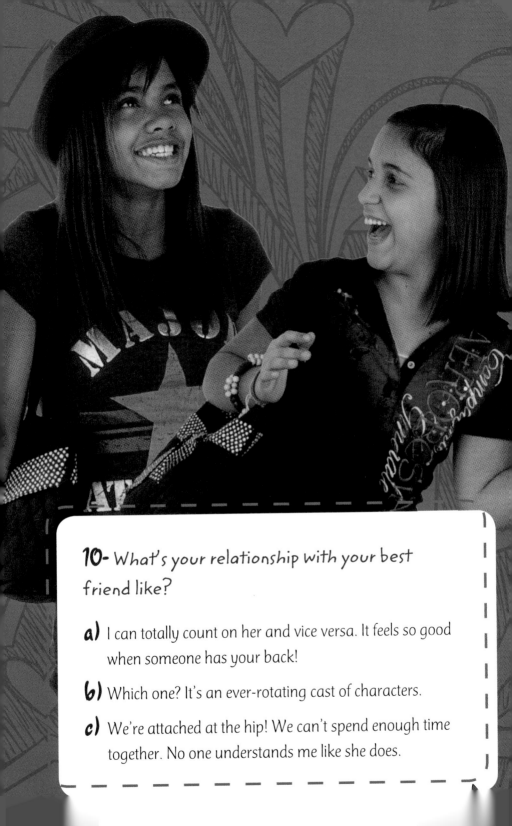

10- What's your relationship with your best friend like?

a) I can totally count on her and vice versa. It feels so good when someone has your back!

b) Which one? It's an ever-rotating cast of characters.

c) We're attached at the hip! We can't spend enough time together. No one understands me like she does.

11- Your big sister accidentally breaks your mom's favorite vase. What do you tell her?

a) "Stinks to be you right now!"

b) "I'll tell her I knocked it over. I don't want you to get in trouble."

c) "Let's go talk to Mom right now. She'll understand it was just an accident."

12- What do your friends love most about you?

a) Your **generosity**

b) Your spontaneous nature

c) Your loyalty

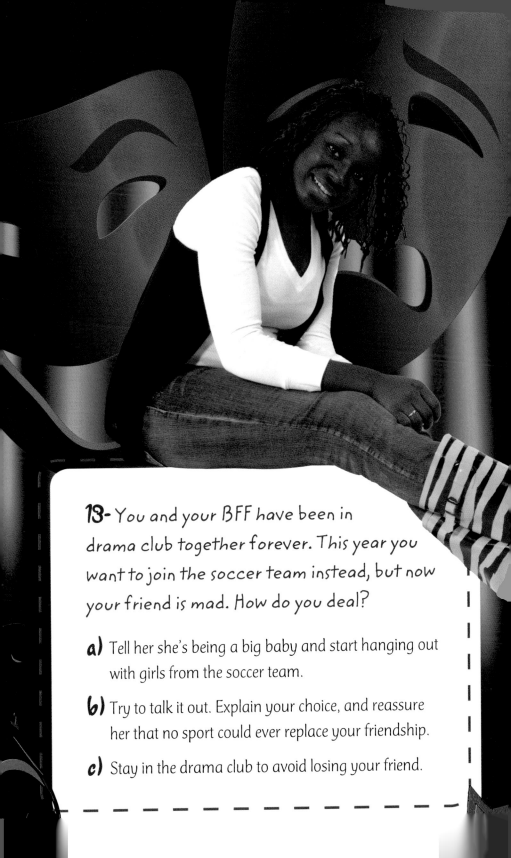

13- You and your BFF have been in drama club together forever. This year you want to join the soccer team instead, but now your friend is mad. How do you deal?

a) Tell her she's being a big baby and start hanging out with girls from the soccer team.

b) Try to talk it out. Explain your choice, and reassure her that no sport could ever replace your friendship.

c) Stay in the drama club to avoid losing your friend.

14- You're shopping with your cousin when she asks you to lend her money for a new handbag. The cost would swallow up most of your cash! You:

a) Say "no way!" You might find something you really want to spend it on.

b) Offer to lend her the money, under the condition that she'll pay you back tomorrow.

c) Cough up the cash without thinking twice. You call it an early birthday gift.

15- Your friends come over for a movie night. You had your heart set on watching the latest movie musical. Your friends are into the new zombie flick. Which one do you watch?

a) Neither. If you can't watch your movie, then you won't watch anything.

b) Zombies rule! A good host always sides with her guests. The musical was probably lame anyway.

c) You offer a compromise. Watch the musical first, then the zombie movie. You have plenty of time for both.

Don't turn the page yet!

It's time to tally your results. Check your answers below. Jot down the number of points you scored for each answer, and then add up your points.

1. a—2; b—1; c—3

2. a—1; b—2; c—3

3. a—3; b—2; c—1

4. a—1; b—3; c—2

5. a—1; b—3; c—2

6. a—1; b—2; c—3

7. a—2; b—1; c—3

8. a—3; b—2; c—1

9. a—1; b—2; c—3

10. a—2; b—1; c—3

11. a—1; b—3; c—2

12. a—3; b—1; c—2

13. a—1; b—2; c—3

14. a—1; b—2; c—3

15. a—1; b—3; c—2

Turn to page 18 if you scored 15 to 25 points.

Turn to page 22 if you scored 26 to 35 points.

Turn to page 26 if you scored 36 to 45 points.

RESULTS

15 to 25 points:

FICKLE PICKLE

Your fair-weather nature could make for a stormy friendship forecast.

The Full Scoop

Can your friends count on you no matter what? Signs point to "no." Sometimes when the going gets tough, you tend to get going. That's not a strong basis for friendship. Being a loyal friend means being able to be trusted. Good friends do what they say they're going to do. They keep your secrets and are there to support you no matter what. It may be time to give your relationship style a makeover. Otherwise your friendships may fizzle fast.

Real-Life Rx:
Tips You Can Use

• Make a list of things you'd want from a friend, such as honesty and loyalty. Then look at it like a checklist. How can you show these things in your friendships? Brainstorm some recent situations you could have handled differently by calling on these **traits**.

• Lost touch with a former friend? Making the first move may be all it takes to refuel the friendship flame! Drop her an e-card, or see if she wants to catch up after school sometime. She'll likely appreciate and return your efforts.

• Don't make promises unless you can really follow through. Staying true to your word is way more important than just telling people what they want to hear. Soon friends will be keeping the faith in what you have to say.

Your Imaginary Alter Ego:
Stacey McGill from The Babysitters' Club

Any Babysitters' Club fan knows that one of the best things about the club is definitely its diverse membership! From Kristy's strong leadership skills to Claudia's creative energy, each member brings something special to the table. And stylish Stacey is no exception. But for Stacey, the very things she once adored about her friends start to become embarrassing after a while. She later decides to jump ship from her beloved BSC, befriending other, more mature friends instead.

What Would You Do?
Girls Talk Back

Get straight-up advice from girls who've been there, done that.

Did You Know?

⭐ A *Girls' Life* magazine survey of 150 guys found that lack of loyalty is a big downer. Among their pet peeves were girls who gossip behind others' backs, whisper rudely, and display other mean behaviors toward friends.

⭐ Even big stars struggle with forming lasting friendships. Loyalty is a rare find in Hollywood. BFFs are always making up and breaking up. On the other hand, some stars form lasting friendships. Taylor Swift has been best pals with Abigail Anderson since their freshman year of high school. Their friendship began way before Taylor became famous.

Q: I went to my neighbor's birthday party. Now my mom wants me to invite her to mine. I don't really want to because I don't think she'll fit in with my school friends. What's a b-day girl to do?

A: The plain truth is that the polite, right thing to do is to return the invite. But there are a few things you can do to ensure smooth social sailing. First, it might be smart to tell your neighbor to bring a friend. That way she won't feel out of place and will have a built-in comfort zone. Also, tell your friends that a few new faces will be joining in—for twice the fun! The more you can set a positive tone, the better the party will turn out.

26 to 35 points:

FOREVER FRIEND

*Your strong faith in
yourself inspires others
to have faith in you!*

The Full Scoop

No flimsy friendships or empty promises
here! Your friends know they have a true
friend in you. It's practically impossible to
break the rock-solid bonds you form
with your friends. And when friction
does happen, you're honest and
upfront! Even though you'll do
almost anything for a friend,
you rarely **compromise**
your own **integrity**. Thanks
to your steadfast loyalty, you
have lots of friends you can
lean on as well.

Real-Life Rx:
Tips You Can Use

• Sure, you're super-loyal, but what happens when that loyalty doesn't get returned? Being betrayed is no fun, but the best way to deal is to go straight to the source. Talk one-on-one with your pal about what happened and how it made you feel. Then discuss whether the friendship can be fixed.

• If you sense yourself growing apart from a friend, you may feel guilty for wanting to move on. Some friendships change and grow with time. That's totally normal! The trick is not to leave your friend in the dark. Share that you'd like to branch out a little and explore other friendships and interests, but she'll always have a friend in you.

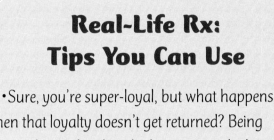

23

Your Imaginary Alter Ego:
Lauren Conrad

OK. So maybe she's not imaginary, but Lauren Conrad also is definitely the real deal when it comes to loyalty. From popular reality star to an author of books for young adults, Lauren seems to live a charmed life. From *Laguna Beach* to *The Hills*, Lauren's friendships were tested time and again. But her loyal, caring nature always shined through. And when the drama cooled down, Lauren remained true to herself, as well as to others. Now Lauren tells her story on the pages of best-selling books that teens love. You go, glamour girl!

What Would You Do?
Girls Talk Back

Get straight-up advice from girls who've been there, done that.

Did You Know?

An online survey found that loyalty was the second quality girls seek in friends. (Good personality came in first!) It beat out qualities such as similar interests and popularity.

Shailene Woodley starred as Felicity in the made-for-TV American Girl adventure. Despite her growing fame and fortune, she remains true to her roots. In an interview, she said, "Life has just been the same [since I became a star]. I've stayed with the same friends and have the most amazing family ever, so I've been very lucky."

Q: My friend has a body odor problem, and people at school are starting to notice. I know I should tell him, but I don't know how.

A: First of all, kudos to you for being brave enough to say something! The fact that you're willing to address a sticky subject for his sake is a huge sign of loyalty. As for how to address it, the answer is kindly and privately. Gently let him know what's up, and that you're trying to save him any future embarrassment.

36 to 45 points:

TOO TRUE BLUE

All you want is to make your friends happy. But does that come at the cost of your own happiness?

The Full Scoop

The good news is you've got a huge heart. You're constantly giving to those around you. The bad news is you're so hungry to please others that it could affect your own happiness! Sometimes there can be too much of a good thing, and loyalty is no exception. It's OK to put yourself first sometimes and still be a forever friend. In fact, your friends might even respect you more for giving that same loyalty to yourself.

Real-Life Rx:
Tips You Can Use

• Do an experiment. Count how many times you say "yes" in a day just because you don't want to let someone down. If the number is higher than you expect, you might want to consider how being a people pleaser affects you.

• One of the drawbacks of being too nice is when others take advantage of your kindness. Is a friend going overboard asking for favors? It might be time for a gentle reminder that relationships are all about give-and-take. After all, being a supportive friend doesn't mean being someone's slave.

• Remember that loyalty is a wonderful trait, and you have tons of it! It's only when you lose sight of your own needs that it becomes a problem.

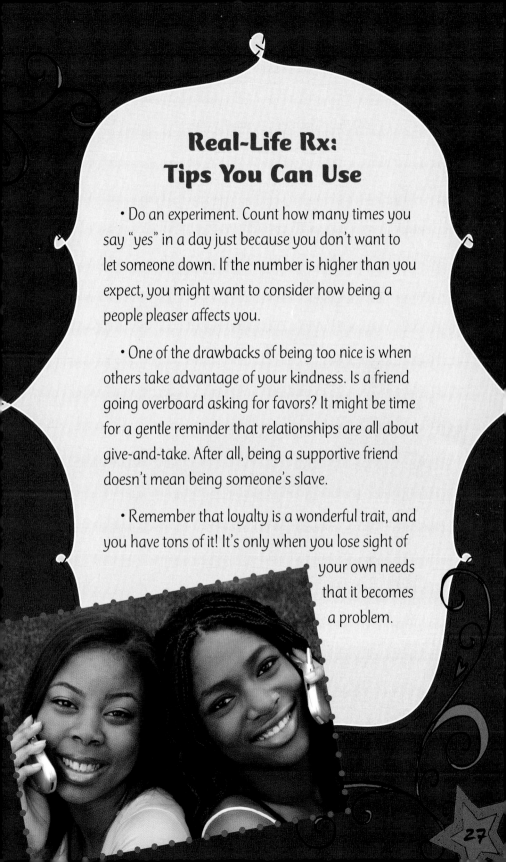

Your Imaginary Alter Ego:
Camp Rock's Peggy Warburton
a.k.a. Margaret Dupree

As sidekick to camp diva Tess, Peggy often goes along with what Tess says simply out of blind loyalty. She's even willing to sing backup in the camp show to help Tess shine in the spotlight. But as Tess' true colors get darker and darker, Peggy realizes Tess is far from a true-blue pal. When Tess finally goes too far, Peggy breaks free and hits a high note as Margaret Dupree.

Even Selena Gomez has admitted to being a people pleaser! She used to have trouble saying no to others, but she's come a long way in recent years. "About two years ago, I started getting better at doing things and making choices that make me happy," she has said. "I definitely feel like I'm getting stronger."

What Would You Do?
Girls Talk Back

Get straight-up advice from girls who've been there, done that.

Q: My friend wants to copy my homework all the time. I'm not cool with cheating, but I don't want her to think I'm a bad friend either.

A: Ask yourself whether she's being a good friend by putting you in such a tough spot. Expecting you to ditch your values and put your own grade in danger isn't really the sign of a loyal pal. Rather than caving to the pressure, let her know that you don't want either of you to get in trouble. She'll have to put in the work—just like you did.

Glossary

cliché (klee-SHAY)—an often-used phrase

compromise (KAHM-pruh-myz)—to agree to something that is not exactly what you wanted in order to make a decision

faith (FAYTH)—strong belief

generosity (jen-uh-ROSS-i-tee)—a willingness to give to others

integrity (in-TEG-ruh-tee)—total honesty and sincerity

spontaneous (spon-TAY-nee-uhss)—without previous thought or planning

trait (TRATE)—a quality or characteristic that makes one person different from another

Read More

Brown, Lauren, Ed. *Ultimate Guide to Surviving Middle School.* New York: Scholastic, 2010.

Lynch, Amy. *A Smart Girl's Guide to Understanding Her Family: Feelings, Fighting & Figuring It Out.* Be Your Best. Middleton, Wis.: American Girl, 2009.

Reece, Gemma. *The Girls' Book of Friendship: How to Be the Best Friend Ever.* New York: Scholastic, Inc., 2010.

Internet Sites

FactHound offers a safe, fun way to find Internet sites related to this book. All of the sites on FactHound have been researched by our staff.

Here's all you do:

Visit *www.facthound.com*

Type in this code: 9781429665414

Check out projects, games and lots more at
www.capstonekids.com

Index